FEELiNG YOUR FEELiNGS

The Head-to-Toe Science of Emotions

Written by Tanya Lloyd Kyi
Illustrated by Phil Nicholls

KIDS CAN PRESS

To my parents. Thank you for teaching me that it's
okay to feel your feelings. — P.N.

Published in Canada and the U.S. by Kids Can Press Ltd.
25 Dockside Drive, Toronto, ON M5A 0B5

Kids Can Press is a Corus Entertainment Inc. company
www.kidscanpress.com

The artwork in this book was rendered digitally.
The text is set in Picadilly.

Edited by Kathleen Keenan
Designed by Barb Kelly

Printed and bound in Shenzhen,
China, in 3/2025 by C & C Offset.

CM 25 0 9 8 7 6 5 4 3 2 1

Library and Archives Canada Cataloguing in Publication

Title: Feeling your feelings : the head-to-toe science
of emotions / written by Tanya Lloyd Kyi ; illustrated
by Phil Nicholls. Names: Kyi, Tanya Lloyd, 1973– author
| Nicholls, Phil (Phil D.), illustrator
Description: Includes bibliographical references and
index.
Identifiers: Canadiana (print) 20240518772 | Canadiana
(ebook) 20240518837 | ISBN 9781525311277 (hardcover) |
ISBN 9781525313516 (EPUB)
Subjects: LCSH: Emotions in children — Juvenile
literature. | LCSH: Emotions — Juvenile literature
Classification: LCC BF723.E6 K95 2025 | DDC j155.4/
124 — dc23

Kids Can Press gratefully acknowledges that the
land on which our office is located is the traditional
territory of many nations, including the Mississaugas
of the Credit, the Anishnabeg, the Chippewa, the
Haudenosaunee and the Wendat Peoples, and is
now home to many diverse First Nations, Inuit and
Métis Peoples.

We thank the Government of Ontario, through
Ontario Creates and the Ontario Arts Council; the
Canada Council for the Arts; and the Government of
Canada, for their financial support of our publishing
activity.

Contents

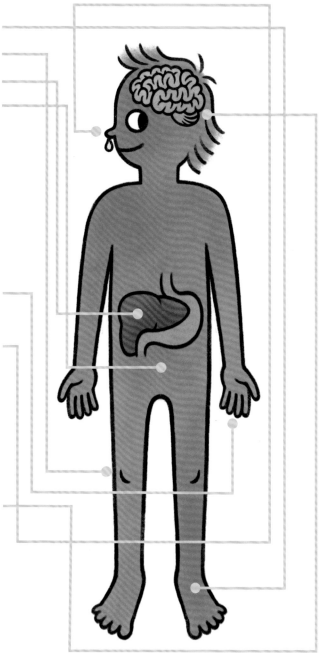

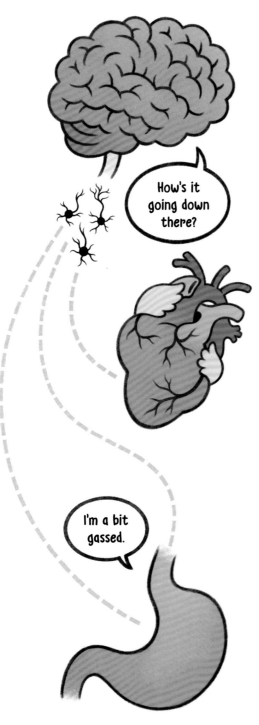

Head-to-Toe Emotional

You've probably heard that your emotions are controlled by your brain. And there's a lot going on up there! You have eighty-six billion nerve cells, or **neurons**, in your head. They gather messages from your senses, memories, hormones and body parts and use those messages to help create feelings.

But nerve cells live in other places, too. There are millions of them in your heart, your gut and even your butt. (Seriously.) While those clusters of cells won't help you puzzle through your math problems or plan your soccer strategies, they might help you sort out your moods.

Every year, scientists learn more about how your whole body helps to process and express your emotions. It's not just your brain — even your tiniest parts get involved. You might have noticed that your fingers and toes move when you're feeling impatient. Your nose wrinkles when you're disgusted by something. And your stomach clenches when you get nervous. That can mean your brain is sending instructions to these areas. Other times, those body parts are sending information to your brain. And your nerve cells are often talking in both directions at once.

How does all this information flow back and forth through your body? And how does it turn into the things you call emotions? Well, that's what this book is about. Every time you turn the page, you'll be taking a close-up look at a new body part and how it might be "feeling."

But you don't have to read these pages in order.

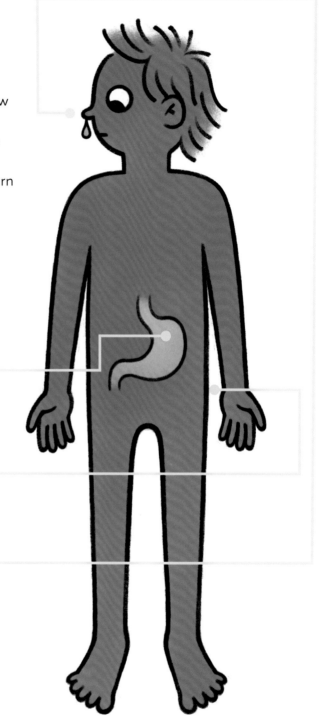

If you have a gut feeling that your stomach might be an interesting place to start, turn to page 14.

If the idea of having a butt brain makes you ... um ... jiggle with excitement, check out page 12.

If you're wondering what's up with sadness and snot, try page 30.

Or, if you'd like a toe-to-head tour of the human body in perfectly logical order, then turn the page.

Let's get emotional!

Stomp Your Feet

Your little brother spilled grape juice on your favorite T-shirt. You're going to get him.

Stomp. Stomp. Stomp.

You won't even need to explain that you're angry. Your brother will know by the sound of your feet. We humans walk more heavily when we're mad. This is true no matter where we're born — Timbuktu or Toronto, New York or New Delhi. In fact, even elephants and rhinos stomp when they're angry.

When you get mad, your body acts like you're under attack. A burst of **adrenaline**, a chemical messenger, sends blood to your muscles and releases extra sugar into your bloodstream. Scientists call this the "fight or flight or freeze" response. Your body is ready for action!

Your little brother probably isn't a physical threat, but your body doesn't know that. This part of your nervous system developed thousands of years ago when people regularly encountered wild animals. And now your body is ready to fight. So even if you don't plan on punching anyone, your stomping warns other people that your body's in battle mode. *Watch out, little brother!*

Stress Test

Have you ever had any of these reactions during a stressful situation?

Hands up to protect yourself

Heart racing to send extra blood to your muscles

Pupils dilating so you can see danger

Lungs working overtime for extra oxygen

Muscles tensing and ready

High-Tech Toes

Video game designers have a problem. Online, people can only communicate by talking or typing. But, in real life, we communicate by widening our eyes, scrunching our eyebrows, folding our arms and puffing out our chests. Without all these physical cues, how can gaming feel as immersive as real life?

Our feet might hold the answers. In 2017, scientists in Denmark asked study participants to wear fancy shoes implanted with vibrating sensors. Then they sent tiny shifts and shakes through the soles, so it felt as if another person was walking on the floor nearby. The participants had to identify different sorts of "footsteps" based on the vibrations they received through the shoes. Were the footsteps aggressive, happy, neutral, sad or tender?

Usually, people were able to identify a definite emotion based on the tremors. Hard, quick tremors felt aggressive, while soft, slow tremors felt more tender. Uneven tremors seemed happy, as if someone was skipping.

Scientists and programmers are still working to fully incorporate this sort of body language, called haptic feedback, into video games. What do you think? Could you get touchy-feely through your feet?

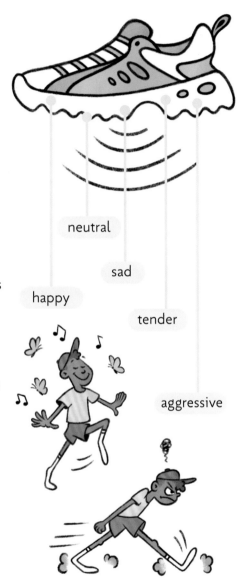

neutral

sad

happy

tender

aggressive

 Want to learn more about anger? Check out the liver-ish lore on page 10.

Or, turn the page for the next stop on our human body tour.

Knocking Knees

Have you ever been so nervous that your legs trembled? Maybe your knees even shook?

Those shivers and quivers are real. When you get scared or anxious, your body sends in the same hormones as when you get angry. But remember, your human stress responses evolved thousands of years ago. You can't run away from or fight a spelling test. (At least, not without talking to the principal afterward.) So, instead, your action-ready knees might shake.

Some of us get extra anxious around other people, especially if we have to walk into a new classroom alone or stand at a podium and give a speech. Imagine you're at the front of the class. Just as you're about to share your research presentation about earthquakes, your knees start to tremble. Soon they're shaking so much it's a seismic event!

Here's what expert speakers recommend:

- **STABILIZE**. Stand with both your feet flat on the floor.

- **FAKE IT**. Hold your shoulders back, as if you're bursting with confidence.

- **BREATHE**. Slow, regular breathing tells your body that you're safe.

- **RELAX!** Those shakes seem big to you, but they're probably too slight for other people to notice.

The good news? Shaking knees don't last very long. The feeling will probably fade once you start your presentation.

What kind of jokes do your knees like to tell?

Knock-knock jokes!

Kneel Notes

From a kneeling position, you can't fight well. You also can't easily run away. By kneeling, you're showing someone else that you're powerless.

Humans use this body-language message in all sorts of ways:

- In many religions, people pray on their knees. By kneeling, they feel as if they're submitting to a higher power.

- In medieval Europe, a soldier would kneel before the monarch and be declared a knight. While kneeling, the soldier promised service and loyalty.

- You need a higher allowance. When you drop to your knees in front of your parents and fold your hands, you're saying you respect them, look up to them and will do anything for a bit more cash!

Here's one last kneel to think about. Imagine a group of students entering a judo dojo. They stop at the side of the mat, facing the sensei (their teacher). Then they kneel and bow. They're not praying to the sensei, and they're not begging for anything. So, what do you think they're saying with their bodies?

 Want to know more about quivery feelings? Turn to page 16 for heartfelt facts.

Or, turn the page for some liver-ish lore.

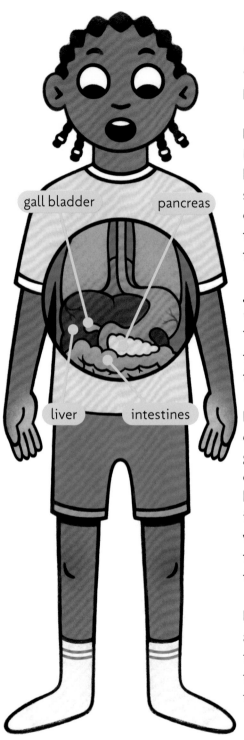

gall bladder

pancreas

liver

intestines

Legendary Livers

Does your liver roil with anger and churn with rage?

Probably not! Your liver is a rubbery glob located just beneath your ribs on your right side. It works with other organs — your pancreas, gall bladder and intestines — to support your digestive system. Modern scientists haven't yet found any connection between emotion and the liver. But thousands of years of beliefs from places all over the world suggest otherwise ...

Playing with Fire

The Greek god Prometheus was powerful and tricky. And he loved humans so much he stole fire from Mount Olympus and gave it to them.

Zeus, king of the gods, was furious! He chained Prometheus to a mountain and sent an eagle to eat his liver. Ouch! But every day, after the eagle gobbled it up, Prometheus would grow a new one. Why the liver? According to ancient Greek beliefs, the liver was the center and source of our intelligence and our most intense emotions. It was sort of like the "soul" of the body. That means tearing it out, again and again, was true torture — for storytelling purposes, anyway.

Strangely, our livers actually *do* regenerate. If you lose a bit of your liver, it will grow back (though not as quickly as Prometheus's did). But historians can't find any evidence that the ancient Greeks knew this. Is the hungry eagle story a coincidence? Or did they understand more than we think?

The Big Boss

In parts of ancient Mexico and South and Central America, the Nahua people believed three organs shared the human spirit:

- The heart was the center of conscious thought.
- The head held people's intelligence.
- The liver held passion and anger.

Mictlantecuhtli, the Aztec god of the dead, is sometimes shown with a giant liver hanging from his midsection.

conscious thought

intelligence

Your Daily Dose

Physiologists are doctors who study our organs and the ways they work together. According to science, your liver doesn't control your emotions. But it does turn your food into sugar for your body and brain. It uses protein to build new blood cells, muscles and nerve cells. It filters toxins from your bloodstream. It even stores important vitamins. If your liver didn't work properly, you'd feel terrible: sick and weak and tired.

So maybe those ancient doctors were on to something.

passion and anger

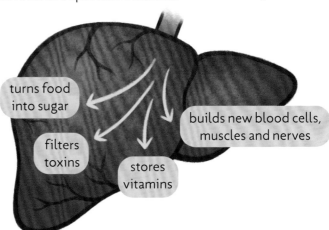

turns food into sugar

filters toxins

stores vitamins

builds new blood cells, muscles and nerves

For more from the ancient world, try some deep breathing exercises on page 18.

Or, keep reading to learn the secrets of the sacrum.

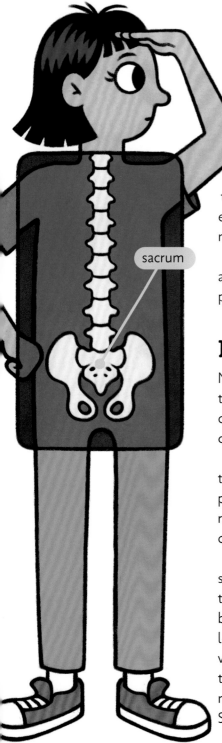

sacrum

What's a Sacrum?

Do you know where your sacrum is? Well, you might not have one ... yet.

There are five vertebrae, or backbones, at the base of your spine. When you're between 18 and 30 years old, these bones fuse to become your sacrum, a single triangular bone where your spine meets your pelvis. But even now, those individual bones are helping you twist, move and stabilize.

People in some cultures believe the base of the spine is also the center of your emotions. And scientists now think people's spines might be "feeling" more than they realize.

Energy Boost

Many Buddhist and Hindu texts speak of "chakras" within the body. They are centers of energy. (The word *chakra* comes from "wheel" or "cycle" in Sanskrit, the ancient root of many Asian languages.)

One of the most powerful chakras lies at the base of the spine, near the sacrum. It's called Svadhisthana. Some people believe that strong emotions come from that region — they say it's responsible for creativity, desire and confidence.

Scientists know that the bony bit at the base of your spine *does* help protect a whole bundle of nerves. And those nerves carry messages back and forth between your brain and your muscles. Sometimes, your brain and your lower body work together to express emotions — like when you're tapping your toes to happy dance music or tiptoeing through a scary haunted house. Those signals run to and from your legs directly *through* your sacrum. So maybe it's an emotional center after all.

Butt Brain

In the late 1800s, when Yale paleontologist Othniel Charles Marsh discovered the first stegosaurus remains in Colorado, he noticed a large cavity at the base of the spine. It was 20 times larger than the tiny space in the stegosaurus's skull, so Othniel started to wonder ... Maybe the dinosaur's main brain was in its butt!

Since then, other paleontologists have discarded his idea. They think the space actually held an organ that helped the creature stay balanced or a nerve junction that helped send messages from the hind legs to the brain.

(If you could have an extra organ at the base of your spine, what would you want it to do?)

Why is your sacrum sad?

It's the butt of every joke.

Was that my butt thinking?

 Like the sacrum, your spine carries all sorts of emotional info. To find out more, turn to page 24.

turn to page 24

Or, go with your gut and flip the page.

Butterflies in the Belly

I'm so nervous, I have butterflies in my tummy.

Whenever I think about the dentist, I have a sinking feeling in my stomach.

It's a gut-wrenching movie. Wait until you see the twist!

Sound familiar? The way we talk suggests that we feel anxiety and fear in our stomachs. Is this just a quirk of the English language? Or do we really use our guts to feel?

The Gut–Brain Connection

Researchers talk about the **microbiome** in the human digestive tract. And you might know from science class that a biome is a big community of plant and animal life that lives in a specific area. So ... is there really wildlife living in our guts?

Sort of! Inside your stomach and intestines are microscopic bacteria, viruses and fungi. If you could take all those organisms from your body and squish them together, they'd weigh more than a soccer ball.

Those tiny creatures are useful: They help us digest our food, fight invading viruses and balance our emotions. Research shows that people with a good balance of different organisms in their gut feel happier and healthier.

People sometimes take **probiotics** — pills or powders meant to introduce new, helpful bacteria to the human body. Could new, microbiome-balancing medications one day help people with more serious mental-health issues, such as depression and anxiety? Maybe! Many doctors and scientists are at work right now trying to figure that out.

If someone's gut biome is really out of balance, doctors might recommend a fecal transplant. They take a healthy person's poop and use a tube to ... um ... insert it into the sick person's large intestine. The new poop can help balance the biome, sometimes more effectively than more traditional medication.

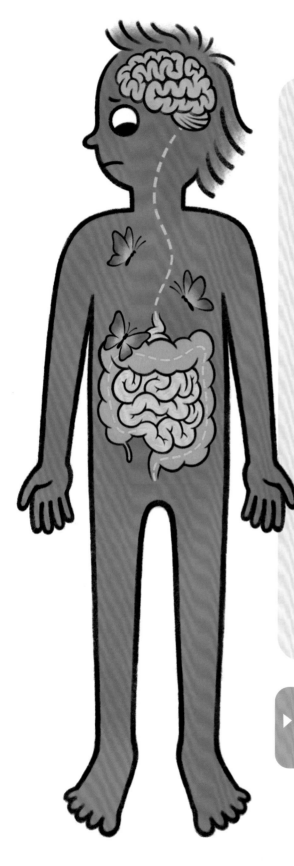

Nervous Chitchat

Sometimes we call nerve cells "brain cells" because there are billions of them in the brain. But there are another half billion in your gut! They were discovered in 2010 by Diego Bohórquez, a Duke University neuroscientist.

There are even nerve cells in your butt. In your colon, to be exact. Your colon, or large intestine, is a tube between your small intestine and your rectum (also called your ... well, you know). The nerve cells there help move your intestinal muscles and keep your poop going in the right direction. They also exchange messages with the brain through the nerve cells of the spinal cord. Some of those messages are about obvious things, like whether you need to use the toilet. But other messages might be about your health and your emotions. Scientists don't yet know exactly what our butt brains are saying. (Eventually, they might squeeze out the answer.)

For more poop facts, turn to page 31.

Or, keep reading to get to the heart of your emotions.

Heartache and Heartbreak

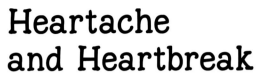

When something sad happens, you might feel an ache in your chest. But why?

Some researchers think we feel sadness in our chests because of the way our language works. Our whole lives we've heard people talking about heartbreak and heartache, so that's where we expect to feel pain when we're sad. But that doesn't fully explain why people from all over the world, who grow up speaking entirely different languages, all feel sadness in their chests.

The psychiatrist Myron Hofer at Columbia University has a different idea. He thinks that social animals such as humans need to stick together to survive. Maybe our bodies are designed to encourage us to stay close. When we break up with a best friend or move away from our families, the cells in our hearts react to the lack of physical closeness, and that makes our bodies hurt.

You're leaving me? OUCH!

Beating Brains

In 1991, a University of Montreal doctor named Andrew Armour discovered a cluster of about forty thousand nerve cells inside the heart. He called them "intrinsic cardiac neurons," but other people quickly called his discovery the "little brain" or the "heart brain." And research since then has suggested that these cells have their own ways of learning, reacting and even storing memories.

Here's one theory: Your heart brain helps you react quickly to stress. To leap from the path of an oncoming car, you need blood to reach your muscles very quickly! It takes too long to send a message all the way to the brain.

Why not ask the heart brain for some extra-quick blood pumping?

Scientists are investigating another theory, too. Maybe the nerve cells in our hearts actually help us feel things. After all, the heart sends messages to the brain and to different body parts through chemicals and nerve impulses. It even creates its own love hormone, called **oxytocin**, which helps people bond with others. For a long time, doctors thought oxytocin was only produced in the brain. Nope! The heart makes its own.

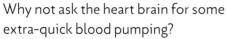

Triple Team

All three of your "brains" — your guts, your heart and your head — are connected by the super-sized **vagus nerve**, a message-carrying freeway. It extends down your spine from your brain, branches out around your heart and then stretches all the way to your large intestine. So even though you might think of your guts, heart and head as separate parts of your body, they're interconnected. And when people talk about their logical brains, their emotional hearts and their gut feelings helping them make decisions, they're not just speaking poetically. They might be scientifically right!

For more about the nerve-cell messages zooming through your body, zip to page 24.

▶ Or, turn the page for some breathtaking facts.

Look out!

On it!

Breathtaking News

No one knows exactly when the *Bhagavad Gita* was written — probably more than two thousand years ago. But the ancient Hindu scripture has plenty of wisdom for the modern world. It talks about philosophy, war and decision-making. And it talks about breath. According to the text, controlling our breath can help regulate our life energy.

Today, millions of people around the world practice *pranayama*, or breath control, in yoga classes and meditation sessions, classroom **mindfulness** minutes and hospital counseling sessions. And scientists are learning more and more about the ways controlling our breath can soothe our bodies and calm our brains.

Breath Control

You've heard of computer control centers. But did you know you have a control center for your breath? It's called the **pre-Bötzinger complex**, or the preBötC for short. Its job is to keep you breathing in and out at a rate that gives your body enough oxygen.

Sounds simple, right? But the way you breathe needs to constantly change. If you're relaxed, lounging in front of the TV watching a hockey game, your preBötC keeps you calmly breathing in and out. But what if your team scores and you leap around the room and cheer? You need extra oxygen to power your celebration, so your breathing control center receives messages from your body and from different parts of your brain and then speeds up your breathing.

You might also breathe faster if you're scared or anxious … or even if you're madly in love! So, your control center receives emotional messages, too. Scientists think there might be specific networks of cells designed to detect different feelings and adjust your breath accordingly. If you're anxious and excited about going on a roller coaster, these nerve cells might detect your brain's jangly messages and your body's jittery ones. In response, the preBötC orders your lungs to work harder — you need more oxygen to help manage that extra excitement.

If you live to be 80 years old, you'll have breathed in and out half a billion times.

Breathwork

You can try these breath experiments for yourself.

· Take long, slow breaths. Each time you exhale, say the word "relax" in your head. After two or three minutes, do you feel more calm?

· Inhale for four counts. Hold your breath for four. Exhale for four. Then wait for four counts before starting again. After a few cycles, what do you notice?

· When you're lying in bed, take long, slow breaths. Each time you exhale, relax a different body part. First your toes, then your ankles, then your calves … all the way to your head. How do you feel? (You might be asleep by now!)

 Turn back to page 10 or 12 for other ancient beliefs about your body.

Or, turn the page for more about lungs … and laughter.

Laugh Track

How many different laughs do you have? There's the polite ha-ha for a silly joke. There's the uncontrollable squeal when someone tickles you. And there's the accidental snort when you're laughing so hard your belly hurts. You can probably think of other types, too. But why does it seem like happiness bubbles from the lungs?

Gigglegrams

Humans are super social. You need to get along with your family members, your neighbors and the participants in your competitive toenail-growing club. You need ways to signal to all those people that you're a nice person. Thousands of years ago, people also needed ways to tell strangers that their toenails weren't dangerous.

The answer: laughter. It's an outward sign that you're feeling good and that you're friendly.

Happiness Hacks

Our bodies have two main happiness chemicals: **dopamine** and **serotonin**. Among other things, dopamine manages rewards — when you accomplish something, dopamine helps you feel great about it. Serotonin also has more than one job, but scientists think the main one is to help you process your emotions, keeping you alert and feeling positive about the world.

When you're feeling great, those two chemicals flow into your brain and bind to tiny receptors there. Then, they set off a whole system of reactions in your body. You smile. You breathe a little more quickly. You might jump for joy or giggle uncontrollably.

So, something makes you happy, then your brain releases chemicals, then those chemicals make you feel happier ... If this seems like a circle, it is! And you can sometimes trick your brain into releasing extra happiness chemicals by *pretending* to have fun. Try a game called Chuckle Bellies. Get a group of friends together and ask everyone to lie on their back. Rest your head on a friend's stomach, and have another friend rest their head on your stomach, until you're all connected. Now ... start laughing! At first, your efforts might feel fake. But as your head jiggles and you hear your friends giggle, your laughs will become real.

You can trick your brain into being happy in other ways, too. Chatting with a loved one, playing with a pet or exercising outside will all help you produce dopamine and serotonin.

Rat laughter is so high-pitched that we can't hear it with our human ears. So how do scientists know that rats can giggle? They tickle them and record the results.

HA HA HA

HA HA

HA HA HA

To go from laughing to crying, flip to page 32.

Or, find facts that get under your skin on the following page.

Skin Deep

Imagine you're called up on stage in front of the whole school. You've won an award — congratulations! But on the way across the stage ... WHOOPS! You trip, slip and dip. While none of this had anything to do with your skin, your face is probably red like a big, humiliated tomato.

Embarrassment is a kind of stress. And when you get stressed, your brain sends a whoosh of extra blood to your extremities in case you need to fight or run away. Some of that extra blood rushes to the many tiny blood vessels in your face. Those vessels are wider than in other places and closer to the skin. So, your body's response to the stress of embarrassment is blushing. Um ... thanks, skin?

Our skin doesn't just show embarrassment and stress. It prickles with fear, shivers with excitement and — according to recent science — helps us "listen" to other people's emotions.

Give Me Some Skin

Your friend is upset.

She's going to share why, and you're going to try to understand how she's feeling. Well, she should touch your arm while she talks. If she does, you'll be better able to interpret the emotions in her voice and truly feel what she's feeling.

Does that seem strange? After all, your skin can't hear!

German scientists Annett Schirmer and Thomas Gunter did a series of experiments in 2017. The result? They found special nerve cells in our skin that communicate with our brains.

In 2018, a French scientist named Aline Bertin noticed that macaws' cheeks turned red when their owners paid attention to them. This "blushing" might be the macaw version of a smile — Aline's planning more studies to find out.

Annett and Thomas observed apes spending a lot of time grooming and petting one another — more time than they needed just to stay clean. Somehow, all that touching was helping the apes bond.

Would it work the same way with humans?

Yes! Using **electrodes** to read people's brain activity, the scientists could "see" reactions to emotions. When people heard an emotional voice and felt a touch on their arm at the same time, they better understood the emotion the speaker was feeling.

So your skin helps you bond with others! But this only works when someone's touching the hairy parts of your skin — your arm, for example. Touching your palm doesn't work the same way. Only that perfect hair/skin combination lets you access those special super-listener nerve cells.

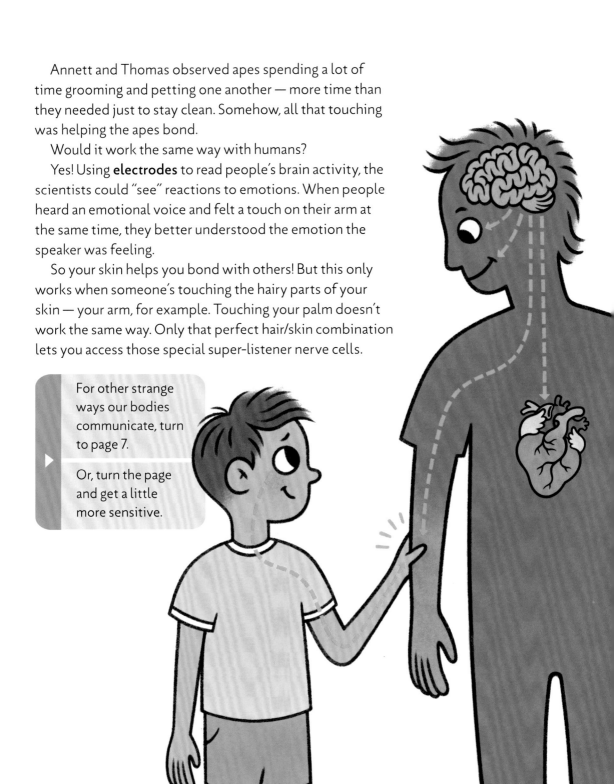

For other strange ways our bodies communicate, turn to page 7.

Or, turn the page and get a little more sensitive.

The Nerves Know

When something lightly brushes against your arm, the nerve cells in your skin spring into action. They signal the nerve cells beside them, and those nerve cells signal the next, which creates a giant chain all the way through your body, up your spine and to your brain. When your brain gets the message (in about 10 milliseconds), it considers the input from all your other senses. Then it sends a message back down the spinal cord: *Spider! Get it off! Get it off!*

Or maybe something nicer: *Oooh ... Epic crush! Stay close!*

HUH?

Sensory Superhighway

Perception is your ability to understand things through your senses. But you have a whole other system that you might not think about: **interoception**.

That's your sense of how things are going inside your body. Is your heart racing? Are you breathing quickly? Is your tummy unsettled?

Your spine constantly carries messages to your brain from both your outside sensory system and your inside one. And by coordinating signals from the two, your spine, brain stem and brain help you make the best decisions.

YIKES!

Spiney Senses

If you injure your spinal cord, you might have trouble walking. But would you have trouble *feeling*?

For years, people with spinal injuries said they felt love, excitement and other emotions differently than they did before their injuries. Scientists assumed this was because people were depressed or angry after their accidents. But recent experiments have shown something different. Without the spinal cord constantly carrying messages back and forth between body and brain, the brain doesn't process emotions in quite the same way.

Imagine you're walking down the street and you spot your biggest celebrity crush. Your heart rate speeds up. Your palms get sweaty. Your spinal cord is saying to your body, "Oooh ... I like that person." At the same time, messages travel the other way. "Everything's going all jittery!" says your body to your brain. Those messages flying back and forth reinforce one another, and you end up feeling everything more intensely.

Now that scientists know how this works, they understand that people with spinal cord injuries "feel" differently. A person with a spinal cord injury might react more strongly to the sight of a person's smile or a waft of their perfume. Their emotional signals travel different pathways.

Fortunately, our brains are great at building new pathways when needed — something scientists call **neuroplasticity**. (You can read more about this on page 42.) As scientists learn more about our nerves, maybe they can help people with injuries create new emotional networks more quickly.

 Head to page 42 to learn how your brain is like plastic.

Or, turn the page for some nerve-wracking, nail-biting facts.

Nail Biters

It's almost time for your piano recital. Your instructor introduces you, and the audience applauds. Your eyes and ears pass that information to your brain, which sends a signal down your spinal cord through the nerve cells in your arms and tells you to ...

Bite your nails.

Wait ... what? How is biting your nails going to help you play the piano under pressure? Sometimes, our emotional reactions aren't easy to understand.

History Buffs

In the 1800s, the psychoanalyst Sigmund Freud said he could explain nail biting. It was a result of too much breastfeeding when people were babies. Or maybe too little. Or maybe people were still too attached to their mommies.

Nope. Sigmund's nail-biting theories became super famous, but they were eventually proven false.

Other researchers thought nail biting was a sign that people disliked themselves. It was a tiny method of self-harm. But that theory didn't hold up either. Nail biters often dislike their habit, but they don't necessarily dislike themselves.

In 2016, University of Quebec researcher Sarah Roberts noticed that people chewed on their fingers to self-soothe when they were stressed. But they also nibbled when they were bored. She began to investigate. And Sarah's experiments showed something new: Nail biters were using their habit as a way of balancing their feelings.

WHOA!

Sarah discovered that nail biters weren't quite as good at **emotional regulation** as other people. We all have a comfortable emotional zone — a sort of "at rest" feeling when we're not too excited but not too bored, not too irritated but not too overjoyed. Finding that zone is like finding the center of your emotional teeter-totter.

Nail nibblers seem to use their habit the same way other people use mindful breathing or visualization: to bring their emotions into balance. And now that health professionals know this, they can help nail biters find other, healthier roads to emotional regulation. (Maybe some of the breathing exercises on page 19!)

Why don't fingernails ever get lost?

Because they're always on hand.

The Biting Truth

Are you a nail biter? Don't be too hard on yourself.

- You're a hard worker. Another of Sarah's studies suggested nail biters were often perfectionists with high standards for themselves.

- You can beat the habit. Only about 10 percent of people still bite their nails after age 35. (Experts suggest using a stress ball whenever you feel the urge.)

SQUEAK!

 For more nervous jitters, turn to page 19.

Or, flip the page to get vocal about your feelings.

ANGRY

HAPPY

SCARED

Voice and Volume

How many ways can you say these words?

"Let me tell you something ..."

Can you say them as if you're boiling with rage? As if you're about to whisper a secret? Can you say them as if you have the most exciting news on earth?

Even though you're using the same five words each time, your meaning can change. That's because we use our voices to communicate both words *and* feelings. The feelings part happens through what scientists call "prosody": your tone, rhythm, volume and all the subtle ways your voice shows your emotions.

The Mutter Map

Uh-oh. Oops. Yay. Yikes. Wahoo. Aha!

These aren't words. Not exactly. Among scientists, they're known as "vocal bursts." They're sounds we make without thinking — automatic emotional exclamations. In 2019, Alan Cowen and his team at the University of California, Berkeley made a sort of map using more than two thousand of these vocal bursts from people around the world. They tracked everything from cries and sighs to growls and gasps. Then they grouped the sounds according to the feelings they expressed and came up with 24 emotional categories.

When friends sniff or snort, you understand exactly what they mean. That's because humans have had thousands of years of practice — vocal bursts are older than language. Before people spoke English or Korean or even Latin, they could communicate in coughs and chortles. (Apes still communicate this way today.)

By mapping the sounds and their meanings, Alan and his team showed just how many emotions we can convey. Their map might also be used to help artificial intelligence "translate" human communication.

When we whisper, we use our mouths but not our vocal cords. And we're not the only animals who whisper. Cotton-top tamarins, an endangered species of monkey in South America, whisper to one another when predators are nearby. It took researchers a long time to discover these whispers — because they weren't listening closely enough!

All Choked Up

When you're stressed, your body automatically opens your glottis, the opening between the vocal folds in your throat. That means you can suck in extra oxygen in case you need to shout or wail. But when you cry, you need to swallow. And you can't swallow properly without closing your glottis! When your body's mixed up like that — usually when you're stressed *and* sad — you'll feel a "lump" in your throat. It's not a real lump, though. It's your throat trying to open and close at the same time.

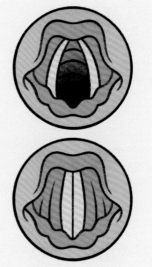

 Keep things humming along by turning to page 36.

Or, take your tissues to the next page for some sniffling specifics.

Snot Spot

Scientists don't say "snot." They say "mucus" instead. That's the official name for the slimy stuff that lives inside your nose and at the back of your throat.

And you have a lot of it. The average person produces a liter (four cups) in a single day. Mucus keeps your tissues moist when they're exposed to air and helps your nose trap dirt and bacteria and then get rid of it. (Handkerchief, anyone?)

But none of this explains why your nose runs when you're sad.

Sniff, Sniff

There's a biological reason for sadness. If you're hiking with your best friend and she suddenly disappears, you need to worry. You can't shrug and keep hiking. You might leave your friend in danger. And you'd be less safe, too, hiking by yourself.

If we feel sadness when we lose something, we'll be more likely to take care of people and possessions we value. We're more likely to stop hiking and search for a missing friend! The ability to feel sad makes us more cautious.

But wait ... none of this involves your nose. So why is it running? Well, your poor nose is an innocent bystander. Your tear ducts release water when you cry. (You can read more about this on page 32.) Some of that water drains through your ducts and into the back of your nose. There, it meets with mucus and creates a slimy mix. You swallow most of it, and the rest pours out your nose.

The Safety Scrunch

Disgusting! If you step in a big pile of dog poop, your nose wrinkles. People react this way in every part of the world — because nose wrinkles are useful.

Doctors call the entrance to your nose the "nasal vestibule." Air passes through that entranceway and into a larger cavity, where it brushes past your smell receptors and then down your throat toward your lungs. When you smell something disgusting, your smell receptors send a message to your brain, which tries to stop more smelly air from entering. Your nose scrunches to try to seal that vestibule. (But you still need to breathe, so it doesn't seal things entirely.)

Try wrinkling your nose as if you just smelled dog poop. Now try breathing. It's a bit harder, right? And it's probably a bit harder to see, too, since wrinkling your nose automatically narrows your eyes.

Some bad smells — or fumes — are dangerous. Some stinky things carry disease. By narrowing your nasal passages and squinting your eyes, you help protect yourself from the stink.

EWW!

Need a deep breath after those bad smells? Try page 18.

Or, keep sniffling to the next page.

Blinking Back Tears

Humans produce three types of tears in the tiny glands around our eyes. One type keeps your eyes moist and clear. The second type keeps them free of debris — these tears will gush out if you get dirt blown in your face. But the third type is entirely different, filled with a mix of stress hormones. That's the type that sends you searching for tissues when you cry.

But why would sadness make your eyes leak?

For hundreds of years, doctors and scientists have been trying to answer that question. And they still don't have a final answer! But they do have a few ideas ...

Crybabies

No one teaches babies how to squawk and wail. They just know. University of Pittsburgh researcher Lauren Bylsma thinks it's probably a reflex — something built into our survival instincts. Babies can't live on their own, so they're quick to ask for help in the only way they can. Baby monkeys, bears and birds demand attention the same way, using some of the same high-pitched sounds.

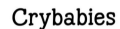

You're not a baby any longer. Are you still asking for help when you cry? Maybe. Some researchers think that crying might be like waving a flag. You're sending automatic messages to the people around you.

Imagine you're having a giant argument with your little sister. You're so annoyed that you'd like to kick her in the shin. (Of course you won't, but you want to.) Then, she starts to cry. Do you still feel just as angry? Or do those tears make you feel a tiny bit sorry for her? Some scientists think that crying is one of the ways we humans solve conflicts and create bonds with one another.

AHH!

Crying might also help people calm down. When you're upset, your heart rate increases and you breathe faster. But if you burst into tears, your body gets back to normal rhythm more quickly afterward than it would if you didn't cry. Researchers still don't know if this has to do with the tears themselves, with the heavy way people breathe when they cry, or with something else entirely. (See if you can decide for yourself next time you have a good cry.)

WAAA!

PHEW!

YAOWW!

Other animals feel hurt or sad. Sometimes, they even make crying sounds. But only humans produce tears of sadness.

 To learn more about surrender messages, knee-drop to page 9.

Or, get a bit mouthy on the next page.

Lip Service

What do you do when someone smiles at you? You probably smile back! And when you see someone crying, you start to frown. When one of your friends is mad, you might grimace — not because you're angry but because you're feeling a little of what your friend is feeling.

It's almost as if your face is a mirror ...

Brain Bounce

In the early 1990s, a neuroscientist in Italy was closely studying monkey brains. Really closely. In fact, he was studying a few specific nerve cells. Giacomo Rizzolatti had noticed something interesting. These nerve cells "lit up" in his scanners when a monkey grabbed a peanut. But they also lit up the same way when the monkey watched other monkeys grab a peanut.

These nerve cells were super specific. They reacted to peanut grabbing, while other, different cells reacted to peanut eating. What was going on?

As they continued to study, Giacomo and his team labeled these cells "mirror neurons." Giacomo suggested that inside our brains, we're constantly reflecting the experiences of people (or monkeys!) around us. As our nerve cells mirror their nerve cells, we feel what they're feeling — literally. So, when your friends are sad, you're sad, too. Mirror neurons help us better understand one another.

Giacomo and his team say these reactions are "involuntary and automatic." That means you don't have to think about whether your friend is frowning or what emotion a frown might signal. You already know.

Game Face

Scientists say we can make thousands of different facial expressions — maybe even hundreds of thousands. If you're a video game creator, that's a huge challenge. You definitely want players to be using their mirror neurons and feeling what your characters are feeling. But it's too much work to illustrate hundreds of thousands of eyebrow wiggles and eye squints that capture all the nuances of real human expressions. How are you going to create characters that look real?

Today's game designers sometimes hire live actors. Using dozens of cameras and sensors, they record the tiniest movements of an actor's face. Then they layer their graphics on top of the actor's expressions for a "real life" effect.

Remember, on page 31, you learned about the way you wrinkle your nose when you smell something noxious? Try this with your friends: wrinkle your nose in disgust. Say "Do you smell that?" See if your friends wrinkle their noses, too. If so, you're seeing their mirror neurons at work!

To learn more about how your feelings are contagious, check out the chuckling on page 20.

Or, turn the page to hear more about sound and feeling.

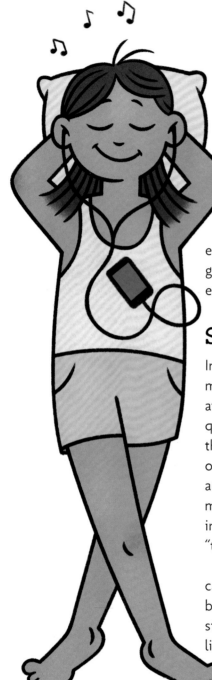

Musical Mayhem

Imagine the final scenes of a movie. The best friend is moving away forever. Cue the violin, the wailing saxophone and the mournful squawk of an oboe. And pass the tissues.

But ... wait. The move is canceled! The friends are reunited. Now chimes ring, flutes trill and piano keys cheerfully clink.

Moviemakers know exactly what music will change our emotions. How do they do it? And why, exactly, is music so good at evoking certain feelings? Our ears aren't centers of emotion ... or are they?

Sounding Things Out

In 2018, researchers in London set out to discover how musical sounds evoked different emotions. They looked at something called timbre — sort of the unique sound quality or "tone" of an instrument. And they discovered that the timbre of emotional music is similar to the timbre or tone of human speech. In speech, angry sounds are loud and rough. Happy sounds are high and pure. Loud and rough music or high and pure music evokes those same feelings in listeners. Though we might not always realize it, music is "talking" to the emotional centers of our brains.

Professional musicians spend hours each day listening carefully to notes and harmonies. Their brain stems and brains actually react differently to sound than the brain stems and brains of the rest of us. Basically, they have listening superpowers. So, if musicians are expert listeners, and music prompts emotions ... are musicians also experts at interpreting *feelings*, as well as notes? Yes!

In 2019, a team of scientists from Mexico and China showed that musicians can hear tiny changes in emotion better than non-musicians.

If you want to fine-tune your feeling abilities, you might want to pick up an instrument.

Sounds can trigger your emotional-alert system.

| You hear an emotional sound. | You scan your friend's face for clues. | You mirror the emotion. | You feel some of what your friend is feeling. |

Emo Ears

Our ears don't move around much, so they're not too useful for *showing* emotion. But other animals use their ears to communicate their feelings. A dog points its ears forward when it's focused, and it lays its ears flat against its head when it's going to attack. Scientists have studied the ears of sheep, horses, goats and cows, and they've learned that all these animals "talk" with their ears, too. The things they say are emotionally *moo*-ving.

?!

GRRRRR

For more about animal emotions, turn to page 33.

Or, keep reading for some hair-raising facts.

YIKES!

Getting Hairy

A couple million years ago, your ancestors were busy evolving from apes. And they were a lot hairier than humans are today. (They had serious back hair. And ear hair. And probably quite a bit of neck hair, too.) But that fur was sometimes useful. If an animal startled them in the woods, their skin cells would contract, and the hair all over their bodies would stand on end. This helped them seem bigger and more dangerous.

Do you ever get goose bumps when you're scared? That's your hair standing on end. But since you're probably not too furry, you only notice the bumps on your arms.

Seeing Red

According to stereotypes, people with red hair are high-strung and dramatic. And when they get mad, they get really mad. There's no scientific evidence to support this. But there is evidence that redheads are more sensitive to pain. Red hair usually comes from a mutation in a specific gene. Over the past couple decades, research from the University of Louisville in Kentucky has shown that redheads are more sensitive to cold and stinging sensations. They're more likely to need extra anesthetic to relieve pain. Probably, the same gene prompts red hair and an extra-sensitive pain response.

You may have read on page 22 about the way we blush when we're embarrassed or stressed. Well, because most redheads have fair skin, everyone knows when they're blushing! This, combined with the extra pain sensitivity, might have led to the stereotype of the extra-emotional redhead.

Tress Stress

When scientists want to test your stress levels, they ask you to spit. Then they measure the amount of **cortisol** — a stress hormone — in your saliva. But what if they want to know about your history of stress?

Well, they can examine your hair. Just as the rings of a tree tell scientists about the tree's age and the forest's water supply and sunlight levels, long strands of your hair can offer hints about the state of your body.

When you're stressed, your body produces extra cortisol. And some of that hormone is captured in your tresses. Were you extra-anxious in kindergarten? Are you more stressed now or then? By measuring how quickly your hair grows, and by analyzing the amount of cortisol at the tips of your hair compared to the amount at the roots, researchers can track the differences in your hormone levels — and your emotions.

Wow, that haunted house last Halloween really scared him.

▶ To get touchy-feely with the tiny hairs on your arm, try page 22.

Or, turn the page to get in touch with your lizard brain.

Hippo, Hypo, Happy

How many words do you know for "happiness"? The language you speak may influence the way you think about these positive emotions. In 2018, a researcher named Tim Lomas from the University of East London published a glossary of positive words from different parts of the world.

- In the Philippines, the Tagalog word *gigil* means the irresistible urge to pinch or squeeze someone you love.
- In German, *heimat* means the deep love of a place where you belong, such as your hometown.
- In Trinidad and Tobago, the Creole word *bazodee* means a bewildering, dizzy sort of bliss.

In English, our most common word for extreme happiness is probably *joy*, which the American Psychological Association calls "gladness, delight, or exaltation" — usually associated with energy and confidence.

So bring on the joy!

Balancing Act

Your **hypothalamus** (hai-po-THA-le-mus) is a pea-sized powerhouse located just above your brain stem. When your stomach's empty, it sends out hunger signals. When you're sweaty, it asks for ice water. And your hypothalamus can also help make you happy. It creates and stores oxytocin, the "bonding" hormone. And it makes dopamine, which helps you feel content.

When you see something exciting or you hear joyful music, the cells in your hypothalamus start to wiggle. They send out chemical messengers to your brain and your body, which make you feel happy. Those happiness chemicals help you enjoy the sights or the music even more, and soon you have a whole happiness cycle happening.

Finding the Fun

We have more complicated emotional systems, too. One of your systems, the **precuneus** (pre-KOON-ee-us), takes charge of storing your emotional memories, deciding how you feel about yourself and choosing which things to pay attention to as you move through the world. It helps you find the things you think are fun. If you're a parkour fan, your precuneus might help you spot ladders and jumps. If you're a gamer, it will help you spot ads for new video games. And some research suggests that people with more gray matter packed into their precuneus might feel happier in their daily lives, maybe because they're better at finding ways to play. (Want to give your brain a boost? Studies also show that people who practice mindfulness meditation can significantly increase their amount of gray matter.)

 Need another hit of happiness? Have the last laugh on page 20. Or, turn the page for more bits about the brain.

Mind Control

Located in the front of your brain, the **prefrontal cortex** is in charge of your most complicated thinking tasks. Need to juggle a soccer ball and recite your multiplication tables at the same time? Your prefrontal cortex will help you out.

Of course, managing emotions can be tricky. You're enormously angry at your teacher for making you take your beetle collection outside? Your prefrontal cortex balances that feeling with the risk of detention and decides that you really can't stick out your tongue at her.

Your Plastic Brain

Your brain can stretch and change like plastic. That's what scientists call "neuroplasticity." If you write rhyming verse every day, you'll start thinking of rhyming words more quickly. If you spend hours a day playing the flute with your nose, your coordination and your music sense will improve. (Um … maybe.) When you practice an activity, your brain builds extra connections between neurons to help you learn and remember those new skills.

Brain plasticity works with emotions, too. When people are anxious or stressed for a long time, that can change their brains and make it more difficult for them to feel happy. On the other hand, the more that people practice understanding and managing their moods and emotions, the better they get. Researchers are studying plasticity so they can help people who've experienced strokes or brain injuries or trauma learn how to better use their brains to manage their emotions.

Feeling Funny

Put your fingers on your right eyebrow. Now slide them up just a little. Nope, that's too much. Down a bit. Yup, right there.

That's your sense of humor.

When researchers hook people up to brain scanners and tell them jokes, that's the area that lights up.

Researchers don't know exactly why you have a sense of humor or why you're (obviously) so much funnier than your friends. They know that we laugh when a common rule of society is broken but it's done in a non-harmful way. Societal rule: Don't mash things into other people's faces. Rule broken in a non-harmful way: chocolate cream pie in the face.

Like touch and laughter, humor helps you bond with other people. Scientists know it can also help you manage negative emotions like disappointment and anger. But there's a lot more research to be done. (Why do dads think that dad jokes are funny? Scientific investigation still to come.)

What do you call a skull without neurons?

A no-brainer.

Not ready for the book to end? Start all over again on page 4!

Or, turn the page and take your feelings to the future.

Conclusion

Ancient Egyptian carvings show doctors studying the brain. Those doctors knew things about headaches and healing, traumas and treatment. But they also believed in gods who controlled human emotions. (Imset was the god of broken hearts — in ancient Egyptian, his name means "the kindly one.")

Five thousand years later, we're still struggling with the gaps between brain science and our own, sometimes illogical, beliefs about emotion. And there's a LOT that doctors and scientists don't know. But every year, they find more connections between our bodies, our brains and our feelings. They're also investigating new things we might be able to do with our heads.

- Could we use microchips in the brain to transfer our memories to other people?

- Could we share joy or excitement with others using only our thoughts?

- Could we "upload" our emotions to computers or robots?

These seem like things from science fiction movies, but they're ideas that neuroscientists are studying in labs all over the world right now.

There's still so much to learn about our bodies and our brains that you have time to grow up, go to university and become a neuroscientist. And then see what YOU can discover about the ways we all feel funny.

Glossary

adrenaline: a chemical messenger that travels through the bloodstream and also nerve-to-nerve through your body. In moments of stress, it helps the body get ready to fight or to run away.

cortisol: a chemical messenger that helps you stay alert under pressure, gets your body ready for action and triggers a sort of sugar rush to give you extra energy

dopamine: a chemical messenger that helps you feel satisfied when eating, drinking or doing fun activities

electrode: a small device, usually metal, that conducts an electrical current

emotional regulation: the ability to notice, respond to and manage your feelings

hypothalamus: an area located deep in your brain, near the top of your spine, that makes and stores hormones or chemical messengers. It helps to balance your moods and coordinate systems such as body temperature and hunger.

interoception: your ability to sense signals from inside your body about things such as hunger, thirst, anxiety or indigestion

microbiome: the collection of bacteria, viruses and fungi that naturally lives inside your body. The microbiome in your gut affects digestion, the immune system and emotions.

mindfulness: a type of meditation with an emphasis on breathing, relaxation and a focus on the present moment

neurons: cells, often called nerve cells, that receive signals from your senses and coordinate between your brain and your body

neuroplasticity: the ability of your brain to change and adapt according to your needs and experiences

oxytocin: a chemical messenger often associated with love that helps people bond with one another and is important during childbirth

perception: the awareness or understanding of something through our senses

pre-Bötzinger complex: a region within the brain stem that helps control breathing

precuneus: an area located near the top and front of your brain that is involved in memory and consciousness

prefrontal cortex: the large area located at the front of your brain that helps you receive signals from the world and decide how to react

probiotics: live microorganisms, often in pill or powder form, that may provide health benefits

serotonin: a chemical messenger involved in happiness, learning and memory

vagus nerve: a large nerve that runs from your brain and along the spinal cord all the way to your large intestine, helping to control many of your body's most basic activities, such as digestion and heart rate

Selected Sources

Alshami, A. M. "Pain: Is It All in the Brain or the Heart?" *Current Pain and Headache Reports* 23, no. 12 (2019): 88.

American Psychological Association Dictionary of Psychology, s.v. "joy," accessed October 26, 2023, https://dictionary.apa.org.

Bylsma, L. M., A. Gračanin, and A. J. J. M. Vingerhoets. "The Neurobiology of Human Crying." *Clinical Autonomic Research* 29, no. 1 (2019): 63–73.

Cowen, A. S., et al. "Mapping 24 Emotions Conveyed by Brief Human Vocalization." *American Psychologist* 74, no. 6 (2019): 698–712.

Lee, Y., and Y. K. Kim. "Understanding the Connection Between the Gut–Brain Axis and Stress/Anxiety Disorders." *Current Psychiatry Reports* 23, no. 5 (2021): 22.

Liu, X., et al. "Emotional Connotations of Musical Instrument Timbre in Comparison with Emotional Speech Prosody." *Frontiers in Psychology* 9 (2018): 737.

Liu, Zhan-Wen, et al. "Liver in the Chinese and Western Medicine." *Integrative Medicine International* 4, no. 1–2 (2017): 29–45.

Manno, Frances A. M., et al. "Uncertain Emotion Discrimination Differences Between Musicians and Non-musicians Is Determined by Fine Structure Association." *Frontiers in Neuroscience* 13 (2019): 902.

Mazzocconi, Chiara, Y. Tian and J. Ginzburg. "What's Your Laughter Doing There? A Taxonomy of the Pragmatic Functions of Laughter." *IEEE Transactions on Affective Computing* 13, no. 3 (2022): 1302-1321.

"Most People Can Identify Fake Laughter." *ASHA Leader* 23, no. 10 (2018): 16.

Roberts, S., et al. "The Role of Emotional Regulation in Body-Focussed Repetitive Behaviours." *Cognitive Behaviour Therapist* 9 (2016): 17.

Schirmer, A., and T. C. Gunter. "The Right Touch: Stroking of CT-innervated Skin Promotes Vocal Emotion Processing." *Cognitive, Affective, and Behavioural Neuroscience* 17, no. 6 (2017): 1129–1140.

Soosalu G., S. Henwood, and A. Deo. "Head, Heart, and Gut in Decision Making: Development of a Multiple Brain Preference Questionnaire." *SAGE Publications* 9, no. 1 (2019).

Tracy, Jessica L., Daniel Randles, and Conor M. Steckler. "The Nonverbal Communication of Emotions." *Current Opinion in Behavioral Sciences* 3 (2015): 25–30.

Turchet, L., et al. "Emotion Rendering in Plantar Vibro-Tactile Simulations of Imagined Walking Styles." *IEEE Transactions on Affective Computing* 8, no. 3 (2017): 340–354.

Venkatraman, Anand, et al. "The Brainstem in Emotion: A Review." *Frontiers in Neuroanatomy* 11, no. 15 (2017): 15.

Vos, Pieter, et al. "The Tell-Tale: What Do Heart Rate, Skin Temperature and Skin Conductance Reveal about Emotions of People with Severe and Profound Intellectual Disabilities?" *Research in Developmental Disabilities* 33, no. 4 (2012): 1117–1127.

Further Reading

Birmingham, Maria, and Katy Dockrill. *Are We Having Fun Yet?: The Human Quest for a Good Time.* Orca Book Publishers, 2022.

Bryan, Lara. *Lift-the-Flap Questions and Answers About Feelings.* Usborne, 2022.

Eamer, Claire, and Marie-Ève Tremblay. *Inside Your Insides: A Guide to the Microbes That Call You Home.* Kids Can Press, 2016.

Habinger, Esperanza, and Sole Sebastián. *Your Brain Is Amazing: How the Human Mind Works.* Orca Book Publishers, 2023.

Harper, Faith G. *Befriend Your Brain: A Young Person's Guide to Dealing with Anxiety, Depression, Anger, Freak-Outs, and Triggers.* Microcosm Publishing, 2022.

Kay, Katty, Nan Lawson, and Claire Shipman. *The Confidence Code for Girls: Taking Risks, Messing Up, & Becoming Your Amazingly Imperfect, Totally Powerful Self*. HarperCollins, 2018.

Kirkness, Tammi. *Why Do I Feel So Worried?: A Kid's Guide to Coping with Big Emotions.* The Experiment, 2022.

Woollcott, Tory, and Alex Graudins. *Science Comics: The Brain, The Ultimate Thinking Machine.* Macmillan, 2018.

Index